CONTENTS

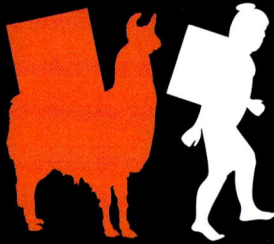

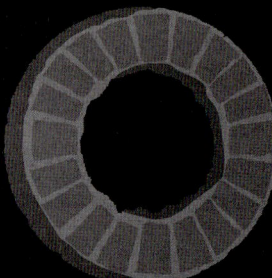

WELCOME TO THE WORLD OF INFOGRAPHICS

Using icons, graphics and pictograms, infographics visualise information in a whole new way!

DISCOVER WHICH MESOAMERICAN PEOPLE CARVED HUGE STONE HEADS.

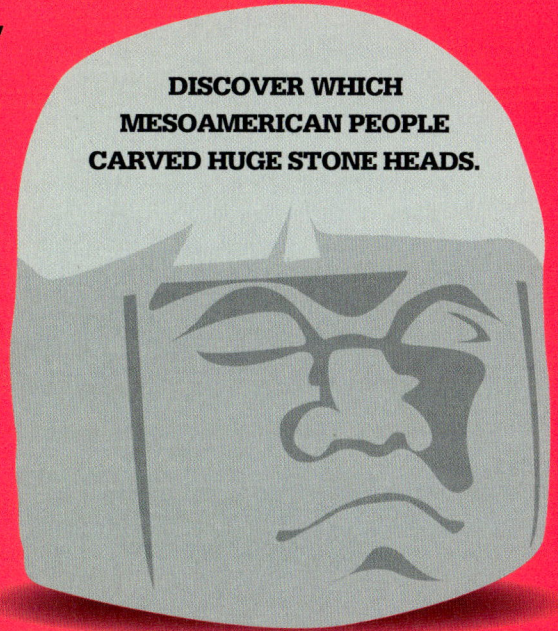

READ ABOUT HOW THE MAYANS WORSHIPPED THEIR GODS.

FIND OUT WHAT WAS EXPECTED OF A MAYAN RULER.

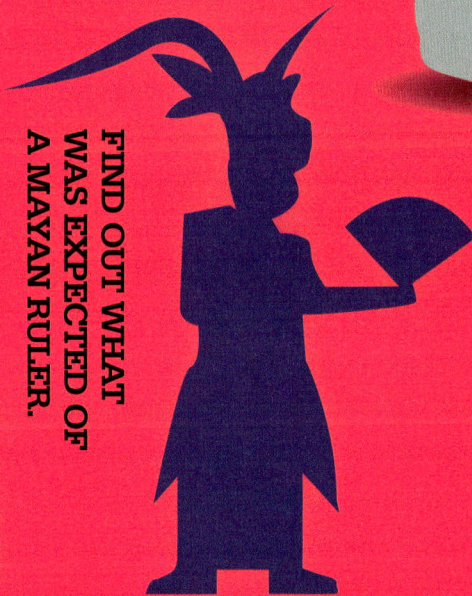

SEE HOW THE MAYANS WROTE THEIR WORDS AND NUMBERS.

COMPARE HOW BIG A MAYAN PYRAMID IS TO THE GREAT PYRAMID OF GIZA.

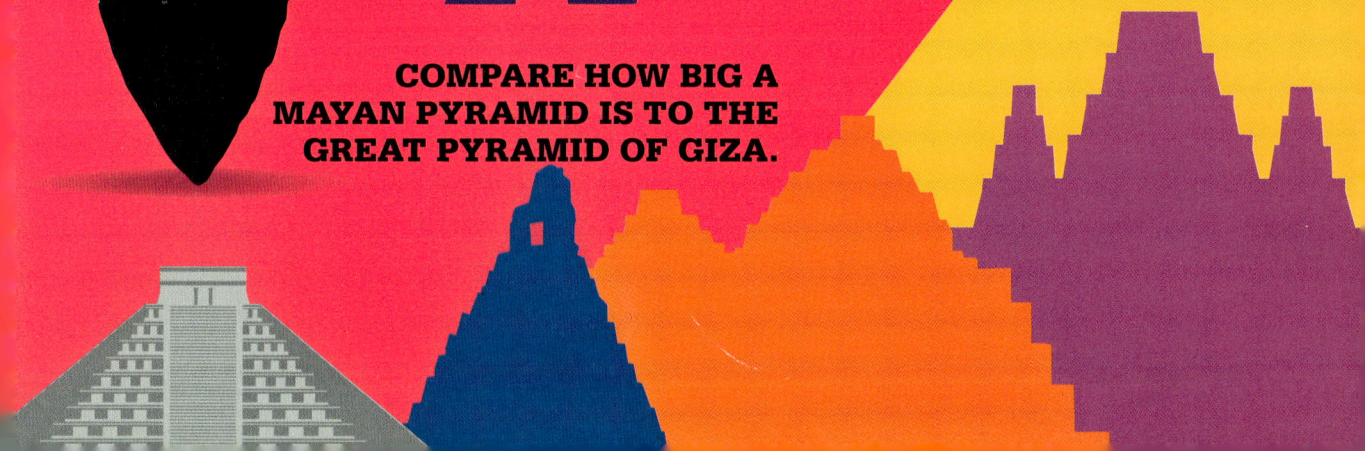

WHO WERE THE MAYANS?

The Mayans were a group of native people who originated in an area called Mesoamerica. By 1500 BCE, they had settled in small villages, but they spread out from about CE 250, creating an empire that flourished until about CE 900.

MESOAMERICA
IS A REGION OF CENTRAL AMERICA COVERING PARTS OF MEXICO, BELIZE, EL SALVADOR, GUATEMALA, HONDURAS, NICARAGUA AND COSTA RICA.

NORTH AMERICA

SOUTH AMERICA

2000 BCE

OLMEC PERIOD
1500–400 BCE

EARLY CIVILISATION
The Olmecs were the first civilisation to develop in Mesoamerica, flourishing from 1500–400 BCE.

STONE HEADS
They are perhaps best known for carving stone heads that were up to 3.5 m tall. That's nearly twice the height of an adult.

UP TO 3.5 M

The name 'Olmec' means **'RUBBER PEOPLE'** and comes from their use of natural rubber, known as latex, tapped from rubber trees.

The tapper scores the tree bark and liquid rubber drips out.

The liquid rubber is collected in cups attached to the tree trunk.

MEXICO

MESOAMERICAN PEOPLES

The Mayans were one of several groups who settled, lived and thrived in Mesoamerica. Some of these peoples increased their power and controlled the region, including the Olmecs, Toltecs and the Aztecs.

YUCATÁN PENINSULA

BELIZE

GUATEMALA

HONDURAS

EL SALVADOR

MESOAMERICAN CIVILISATIONS

- ● MAYAN CIVILISATION
- ● OLMEC HEARTLAND
- ● AZTEC EMPIRE

MAYAN CLASSICAL PERIOD CE 250–900	TOLTEC PERIOD CE 900–1200	AZTEC PERIOD CE 1200–1521	PRESENT DAY

ABOUT CE 250
THE MAYANS START TO ESTABLISH AND DEVELOP LARGE STONE CITIES, SUCH AS TIKAL, COPÁN AND PALENQUE

ABOUT CE 900
THE MAYAN CIVILISATION MYSTERIOUSLY DECLINES

1821
MEXICO BECOMES INDEPENDENT OF SPAIN

2 MILLION

THE NUMBER OF PEOPLE THE MAYANS RULED AT THE PEAK OF THEIR CIVILISATION, DURING THE MAYAN CLASSICAL PERIOD. THIS LASTED FROM CE 250 TO CE 900.

MAYAN CITIES

The Mayans built some of the largest cities in the Americas, from which they controlled huge areas of Mesoamerica. Over time, these cities grew in size, until about CE 900, when they were mysteriously abandoned.

Many Mayan cities were linked by roads, called **sacbeob**, meaning **'white way'**. The longest of these measured more than **300 km**.

The city of Tikal flourished until about CE 900, when it was mysteriously abandoned, possibly due to a combination of forest clearing, too many people and water shortages.

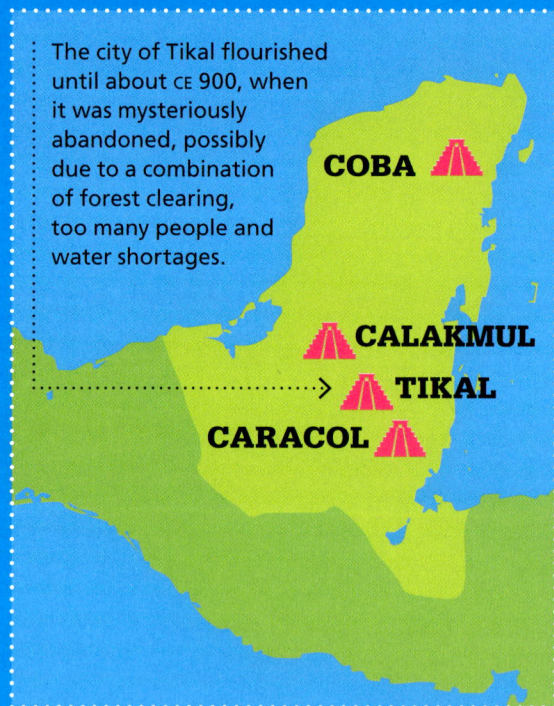

COBA

CALAKMUL

TIKAL

CARACOL

40

THE NUMBER OF **MAJOR CITIES** AT THE HEIGHT OF THE MAYAN CIVILISATION. TODAY, MANY OF THESE ARE UNESCO WORLD HERITAGE SITES. THE RUINS AT CHICHÉN ITZÁ ARE VISITED BY ABOUT 1.2 MILLION PEOPLE EVERY YEAR.

AT ITS PEAK, **TIKAL** COVERED AN AREA OF **130 SQUARE KILOMETRES**, MORE THAN TWICE THE AREA OF THE ISLAND OF MANHATTAN, NEW YORK CITY.

The Mayans may have used **astronomy** to decide the locations of their cities.

NEW DISCOVERY

In 2016, William Gadoury, a 15-year-old schoolboy from Canada, used this theory, along with satellite images, to find what may be the remains of a lost Mayan city. The ruins lie buried deep in the rainforest in the Yucatán. William called this new city K'aak Chi, meaning 'Mouth of Fire'.

CONSTANTINOPLE

CORDOVA

BAGHDAD

CHANGAN

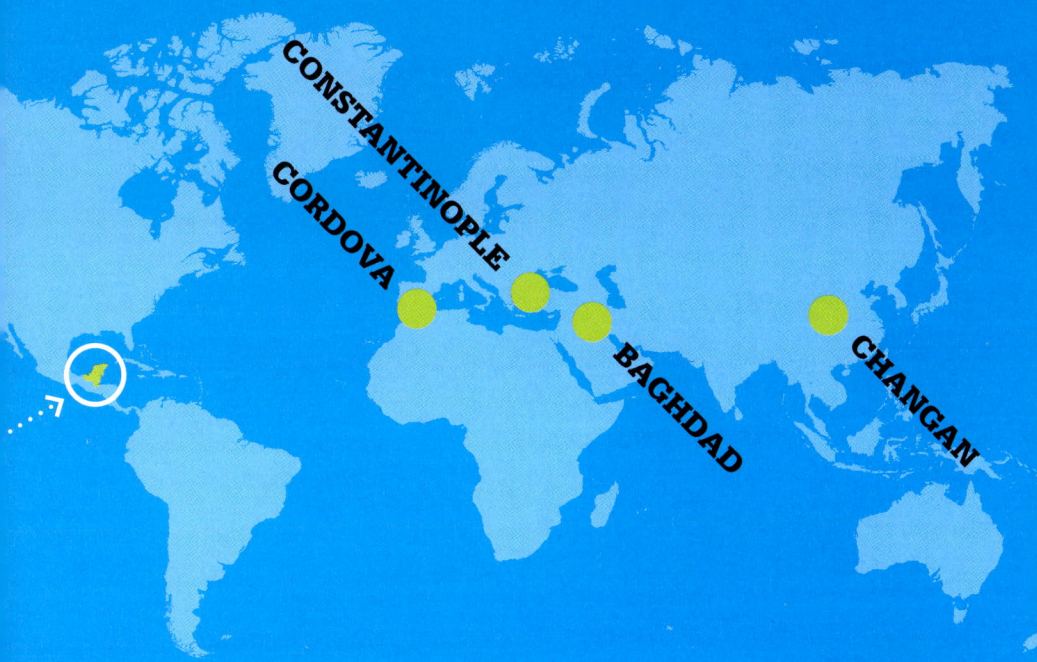

OTHER CITIES AROUND
THE WORLD (CE 900)

Although they were the biggest settlements in the Americas, the Mayan cities were dwarfed by other cities around the world at the time.

BAGHDAD, IRAQ
900,000 PEOPLE

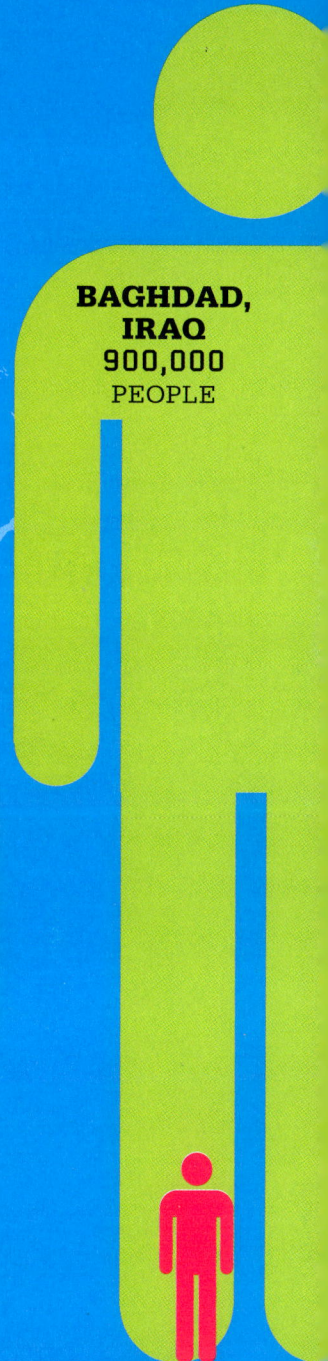

CHANGAN, CHINA
500,000 PEOPLE

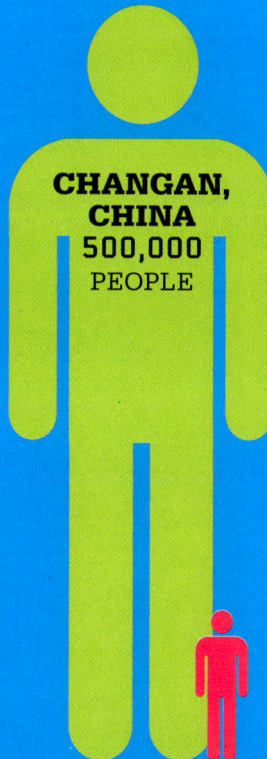

CONSTANTINOPLE, BYZANTINE EMPIRE
300,000 PEOPLE

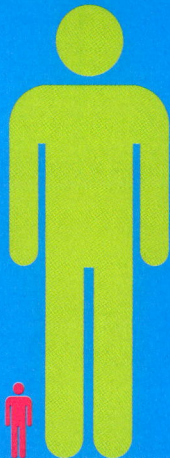

CORDOVA, SPAIN
200,000 PEOPLE

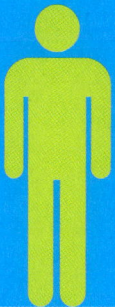

KEY MAYAN CITIES:

COBA
50,000 PEOPLE
(CE 600–900)

CALAKMUL
50,000 PEOPLE
(CE 600–900)

TIKAL
100,000 PEOPLE
(CE 600–900)

CARACOL
140,000 PEOPLE
(CE 250–900)

MAYAN BUILDINGS

The Mayans filled their cities with amazing structures, including huge pyramids, ornate palaces and enormous courts and squares.

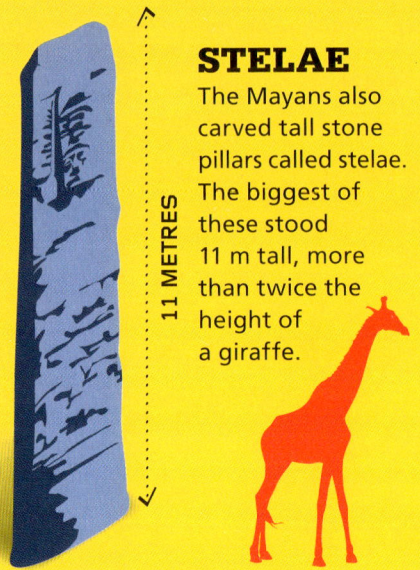

STELAE
The Mayans also carved tall stone pillars called stelae. The biggest of these stood 11 m tall, more than twice the height of a giraffe.

11 METRES

TOWN PLANNING
Mayan buildings and towns were built around a central square, or plaza, and a large palace. Temples, homes and other major buildings were constructed around smaller squares.

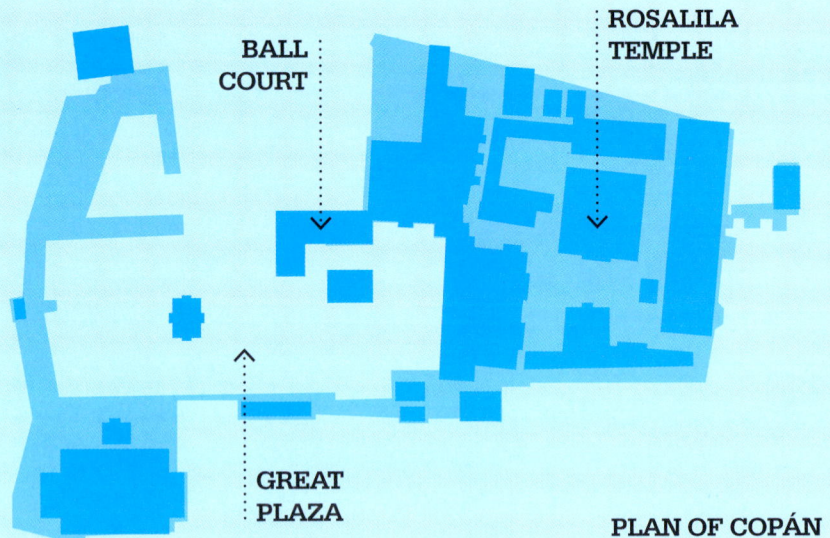

BALL COURT

ROSALILA TEMPLE

GREAT PLAZA

PLAN OF COPÁN

EL CASTILLO, CHICHÉN ITZÁ

Each of the four sides of the El Castillo pyramid, in the Mayan city of Chichén Itzá, has 91 steps. When added together, along with the single step into the temple at the top, this makes 365 steps – one for every day of the year.

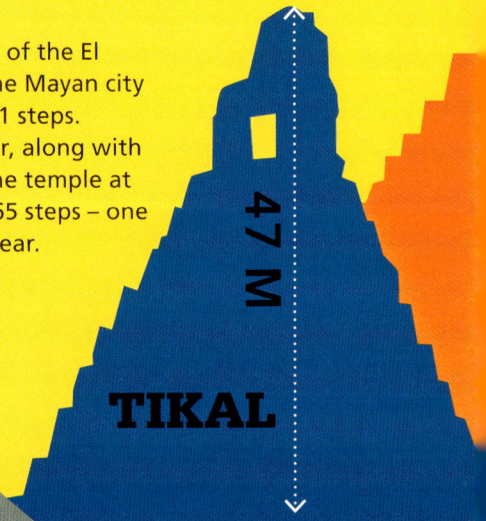

30 M

47 M

TIKAL

THE MAYANS PLAYED A BALL GAME WHERE PLAYERS KICKED OR KNOCKED A BALL AROUND A LARGE I-SHAPED COURT. THE COURT AT CHICHÉN ITZÁ MEASURES 96 METRES LONG AND ABOUT 30.5 METRES WIDE.

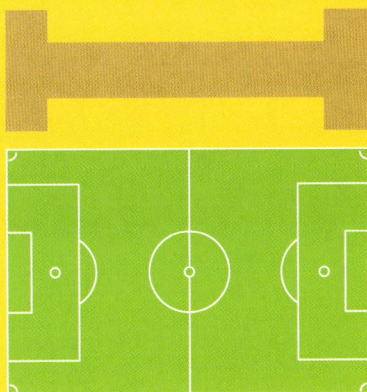

THAT'S AS LONG AS A FOOTBALL PITCH.

TRUE ARCH

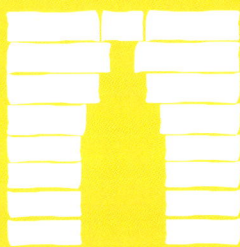

CORBEL ARCH

ARCHES

The Mayans did not use true arches in any buildings. Instead they used corbel arches.

GREAT PYRAMID, GIZA, EGYPT

146.5 M

72 M

55 M

EL TIGRE, EL MIRADOR

LA DANTA, EL MIRADOR

MAYAN BELIEFS

The Mayans worshipped more than 165 gods. Rather than being omnipotent and immortal, many of these gods were like humans. They would grow old and even die, but they still demanded human sacrifices.

THE MAYANS DIVIDED THE WORLD INTO THREE PARTS – **HEAVEN, EARTH AND THE UNDERWORLD.** THESE WERE LINKED TOGETHER BY THE GIANT 'WORLD TREE'.

SACRIFICIAL KNIFE

25 CENTIMETRES

Mayan priests used a **25-centimetre-long** knife to sacrifice their victims.

HUMAN SACRIFICES

The Mayans practised human sacrifice to keep the gods happy. In fact, one of the main reasons they went to war was to capture victims for sacrifice.

SACRIFICES WERE USUALLY PERFORMED AT THE TOP OF ONE OF A CITY'S PYRAMIDS.

BLOOD LETTING

Mayan nobles carried out 'blood letting' to keep the gods happy. They would pierce parts of their bodies using spines or a thorn-studded cord and splatter the blood as an offering.

MAYANS BELIEVED THAT EVERY PERSON HAD A **SPIRITUAL ANIMAL COMPANION**, CALLED A *WAY'OB*. KINGS USUALLY HAD A **JAGUAR** AS THEIR COMPANION AND WERE OFTEN SHOWN AS A JAGUAR IN MAYAN ART.

HONOURABLE BURIAL

Mayan rulers were buried with great honour. King Pakal, who ruled for 60 years, was buried in CE 683 in a funeral chamber at the heart of the Temple of the Inscriptions in the city of Palenque. His sarcophagus contained beautiful jade objects and jewellery.

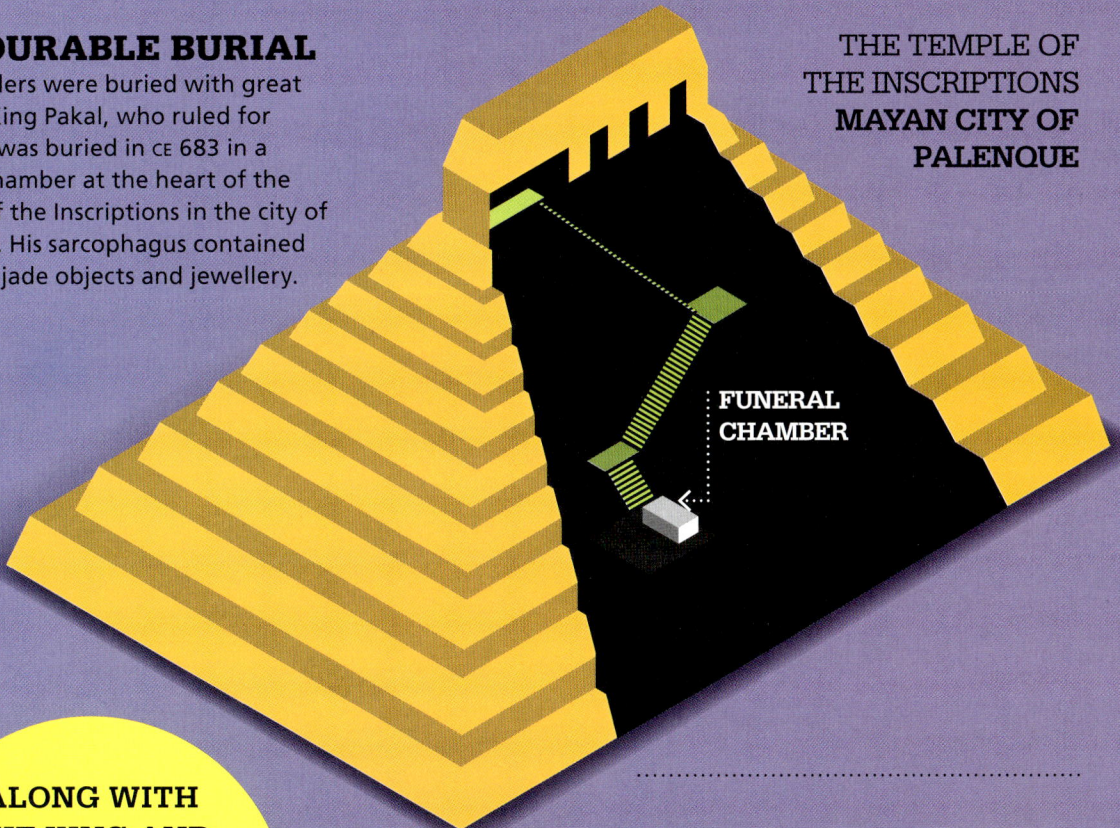

THE TEMPLE OF THE INSCRIPTIONS **MAYAN CITY OF PALENQUE**

FUNERAL CHAMBER

ALONG WITH THE KING AND NOBLES, MAYAN PRIESTS WERE THE ONLY PEOPLE WHO COULD READ AND WRITE.

MAYAN RELIGIOUS CEREMONIES COULD LAST FOR MORE THAN

6 HOURS

COUNTING AND WRITING

The Mayans created complicated systems for counting and recording their observations. They also created a calendar system, which they used to predict events many years in advance.

TUN
STONE

K'U K'UL
SACRED, GOD

KAH
TOWN, AREA

GLYPHS

Around 700 BCE, the Mayans invented a writing system that was based on about 800 different symbols, known as glyphs. These were used to represent sounds, ideas or both. They were usually written in paired columns in texts called codices.

CHAN
SKY

K'IN
SUN

K' AK'
FIRE

HA'
WATER

NIK
FLOWER

BIH
ROAD

WINK
MAN, PERSON

TODAY, ONLY **FOUR CODICES REMAIN.** ONE OF THE SURVIVING TEXTS IS NEARLY **7 METRES LONG** ...

... ALMOST **TWICE THE LENGTH OF A CAR.**

The codices were written on paper made from the bark of fig trees. The paper sheets were folded like a concertina.

0 1 2 3 4 5 6 7 8 9 10 11

THE MAYANS USED A COUNTING SYSTEM BASED AROUND THE NUMBER **20**, CALLED A **VIGESIMAL SYSTEM** ...

THE MAYANS USED A CALENDAR THAT WAS MADE UP OF THREE DIFFERENT CYCLES, CALLED THE TZOLKIN, THE HAAB AND THE LONG COUNT.

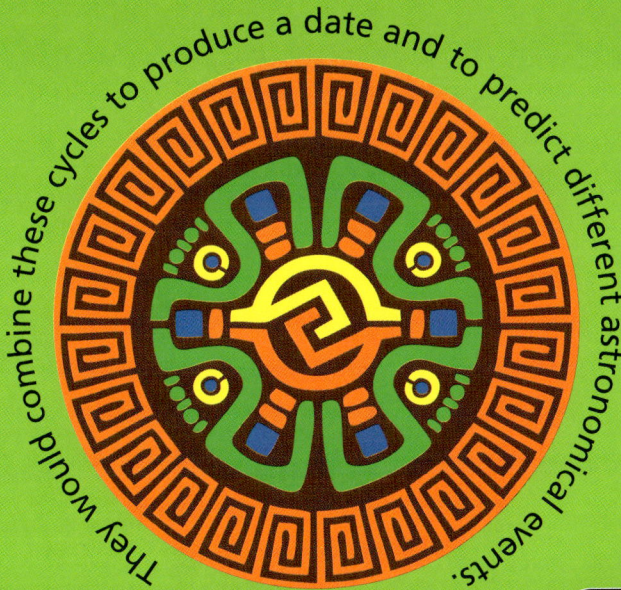

They would combine these cycles to produce a date and to predict different astronomical events.

The Tzolkin lasted for **260 DAYS** and was divided into **20** periods, each lasting **13** days.

The Haab lasted for **365 DAYS** and was divided into **18** periods of **20** days each, with another period lasting just **5** days.

LONG COUNT CYCLE

The Long Count was a star-based calendar that was made up of cycles lasting 2,880,000 days. The Mayans believed that the universe would be destroyed and recreated at the end and beginning of each Long Count cycle.

The Long Count date was spoken about in terms of **Kins, Uinals, Tuns, Katuns** and **Baktuns**:

1 kin = 1 day

1 uinal = 20 kin = 20 days

1 tun = 18 uinals = 360 days

1 katun = 20 tun = 7,200 days

1 baktun = 20 katun = 144,000 days

21 DECEMBER 2012

MANY PEOPLE BELIEVED THAT THE WORLD WOULD BE DESTROYED AT THE END OF THE LAST MAYAN CYCLE, WHICH FELL ON 21 DECEMBER 2012. HOWEVER, NOTHING HAPPENED. THE EARTH SURVIVED AND THE MAYAN CALENDAR CONTINUED.

12 13 14 15 16 17 18 19 20

... THEY ALSO UNDERSTOOD THE CONCEPT OF **ZERO** LONG BEFORE EUROPEANS DID.

MAYAN SOCIETY

The Mayans had a rigid social structure. At the top was the ruler, known as the *ajau* or *halach uinic*. Beneath this were layers of nobles, priests, merchants, farmers and slaves, each with their own roles.

Mayan rulers were married to their mothers at the age of five.

NOBLES

The nobles were made up of local governors and important people who enforced local laws and tax collecting.

MERCHANTS

Merchants traded between different towns and cities – some were even suspected of being spies. Artisans created objects and buildings.

RULER

The position of ruler was hereditary, and passed down from father to son. Rulers had many ceremonial duties and were thought of as a link between the real world and the supernatural.

WOMEN RULERS

Sak K'uk was one of the few women to rule. She governed the city of Palenque between CE 612–615, after her father died and before her son became old enough to rule.

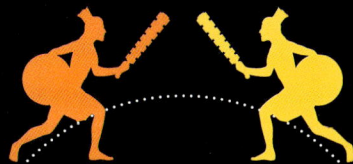

WARRIORS WERE A CLASS ON THEIR OWN, AND COULD COME FROM ANY PART OF MAYAN SOCIETY.

PRIESTS

Priests performed religious rituals, including sacrifices. They also made astronomical observations and predictions using the Mayan calendar.

PEASANTS

Peasants, farmers and slaves made up most of Mayan society, growing the crops that fed the population.

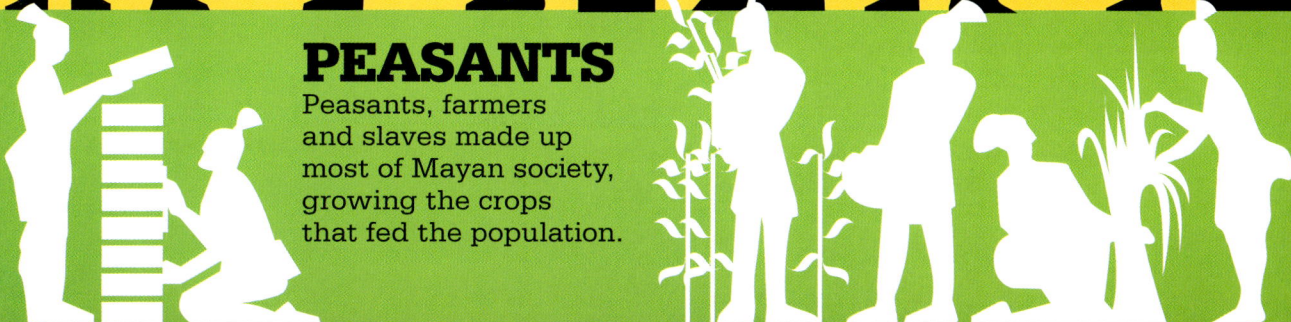

MAYAN WARFARE

The Mayans fought wars largely to capture prisoners they could sacrifice to please their gods. However, as populations grew and resources became scarce, the Mayans fought wars almost continuously to increase the amount of land they controlled.

One **Mayan legend** tells of a defending army throwing containers filled with **hornets** at attacking soldiers. The hornets flew out of the containers, **stinging** the attackers.

LONG-DISTANCE WEAPONS

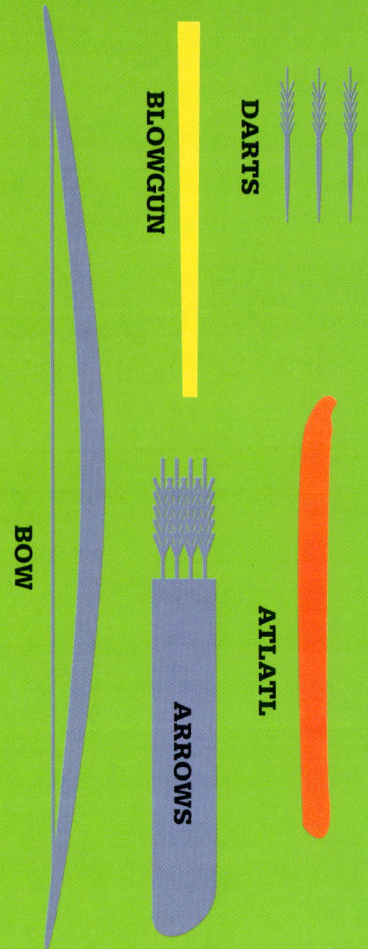

BLOWGUN

DARTS

BOW

ARROWS

ATLATL

HOW TO USE AN ATLATL

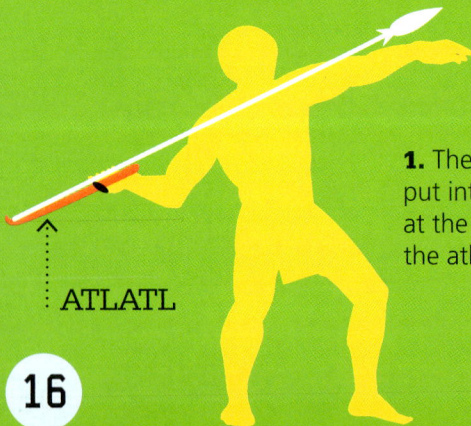

SPEAR

ATLATL

1. The spear is put into a notch at the back of the atlatl.

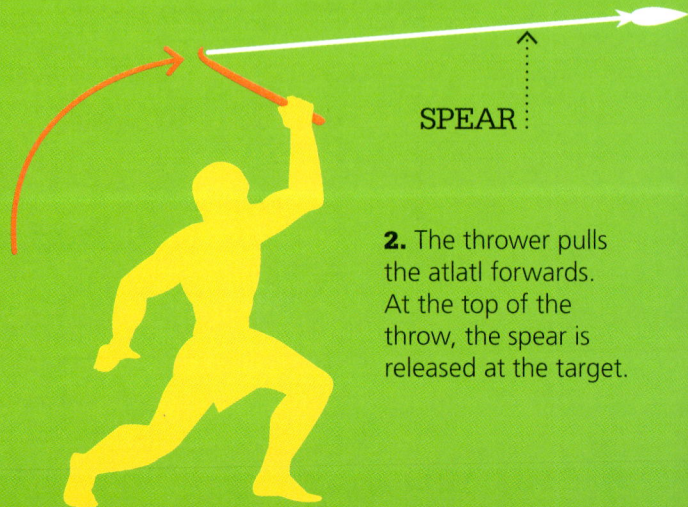

2. The thrower pulls the atlatl forwards. At the top of the throw, the spear is released at the target.

FIGHTING WEAPONS

KNIFE

AXE

SPEAR

ABOUT 1 M

WAR CLUB
was lined with sharp blades made from a rock called obsidian.

ARMOUR
Wealthier Mayans had armour made from thick cotton that had been treated with rock salt to make it tougher.

MAYAN WARRIORS BELIEVED THAT THEY COULD GAIN THE STRENGTH OF A CAPTURED ENEMY BY EATING THEIR HEART.

SHIELD
made from animal skins, reed matting or carved wood.

3. The atlatl increases the speed at which the spear is released, letting it travel farther.

MAYAN BATTLES WERE ONLY FOUGHT DURING THE DAY. IF A BATTLE STRETCHED ON INTO THE EVENING, A TEMPORARY TRUCE WAS CALLED UNTIL THE NEXT MORNING.

FOOD AND FARMING

Growing enough food to feed an increasing population was key to Mayan society. While places in more fertile areas could grow plenty to eat, those located in less fertile areas had to rely on trade to get enough food.

AT ANY ONE TIME, AS MUCH AS

90

PER CENT OF THE MAYAN POPULATION WAS INVOLVED IN FARMING.

MAIZE

Maize was so important to the Mayans that it was central to their creation stories. The Mayan maize god, *Yum Caax* ('Master of the Fields in Harvest') carried the World Tree out of hell, according to legend. The World Tree, which held the centre of the Earth, was often shown as a maize plant.

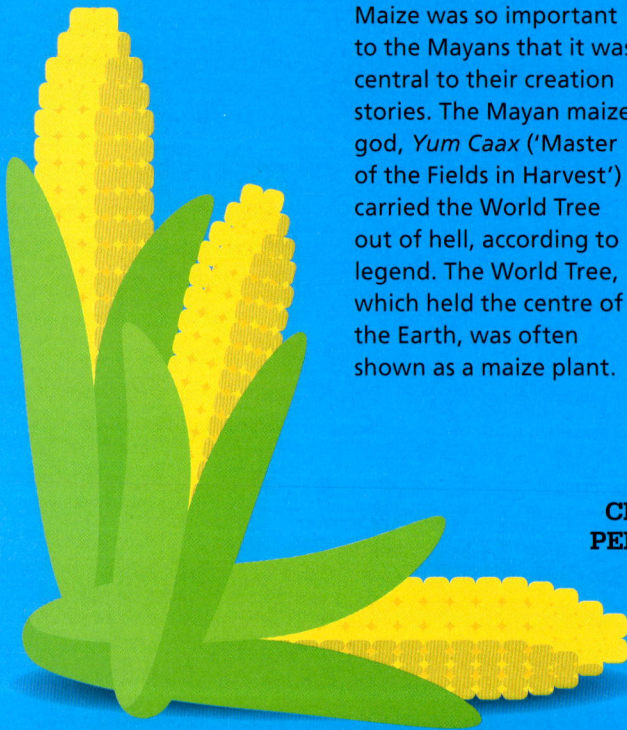

MAIZE

LIME

CHILLI PEPPERS

MAIZE WAS USUALLY BOILED IN WATER AND LIME JUICE THEN MIXED WITH CHILLI PEPPERS AND EATEN AS A PORRIDGE.

OTHER KEY MAYAN FOODS INCLUDED:

DEER

WILD TURKEY

FISH

CHOCOLATE

The Mayans are believed to have been the first people to grow the cacao plant. They ground up cocoa beans to mix with chilli, cornmeal and honey to make a drinking chocolate called *xocolati*.

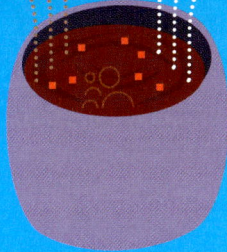

HONEY

CHILLI PEPPERS

FERTILE SOIL

The Mayans practised slash-and-burn techniques, where the forest was burned to the ground and crops could be grown for two years. The land then had to be left for five to seven years to become fertile again. In highland areas, where soil quality was poorer, the land had to be left for up to 15 years.

DIFFICULT TERRAIN

In mountainous areas, the Mayans built terraces for growing crops.

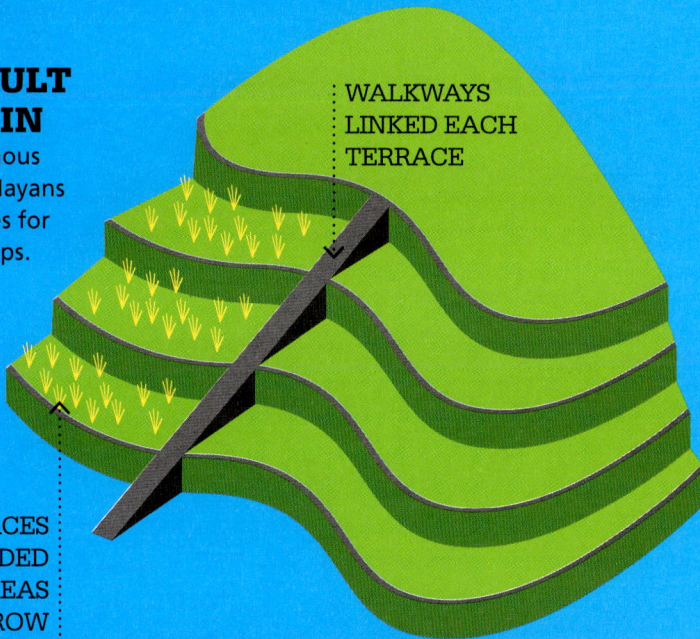

WALKWAYS LINKED EACH TERRACE

TERRACES PROVIDED FLAT AREAS TO GROW CROPS ON

THE MAYANS BUILT IRRIGATION SYSTEMS AND RESERVOIRS TO WATER CROPS, ESPECIALLY IN AREAS PRONE TO DROUGHTS. IN TIKAL, THE LARGEST RESERVOIR COULD HOLD NEARLY 75,000 CUBIC METRES OF WATER – ENOUGH TO FILL 30 OLYMPIC SWIMMING POOLS.

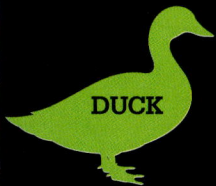
DUCK

EGGS

SQUASH

BEANS

HEALTH AND SPORT

The Mayans developed a number of ways to treat sick people. Healthy people were thought to have all aspects of their life in balance – if one aspect fell out of balance then they became sick. Healers had to find out what had gone wrong and then prescribe the correct cure. In order to stay fit, the Mayans took part in a brutal ball sport, which you definitely didn't want to lose!

PURE BODY

Mayan health and medicine were very closely linked to spirituality. Steam baths (similar to saunas) were used as a way of purifying the body. Piedras Negras, in modern Guatemala, had no fewer than eight stone buildings that were steam baths just for the city's royalty.

MAYAN MEDICINE

Common plants used in Mayan medicine included cacao, tobacco, agave and chilli peppers. The Mayans also used body parts from animals, including insects, fish, birds and even crocodiles.

BIRDS

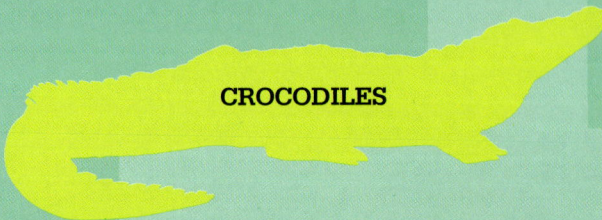

CROCODILES

FISH

CHILLI PEPPERS

CACAO

TOBACCO

POPULAR SPORT

The Mayans played a ball game on specially built courts. Two teams, each containing two to six players, used their elbows, hips and knees to knock a rubber ball to each other. The aim of the game was to get the other team to drop the ball.

THE BALL WAS MADE FROM RUBBER AND WEIGHED AROUND 3–4 KG – ABOUT THE WEIGHT OF A CAT.

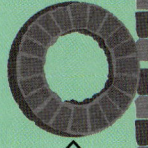

STONE RINGS were located high up the sides in later ball courts. Teams would try to knock the ball through these hoops as well.

DEADLY BALLS
According to one Spanish explorer, the balls could be so hard that players were sometimes killed when they were hit by them.

INSECTS

AGAVE

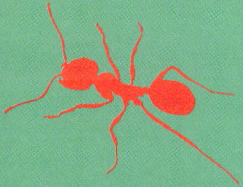

PLANTS WITH DIFFERENT COLOURS WERE USED TO TREAT VARIOUS ILLNESSES:

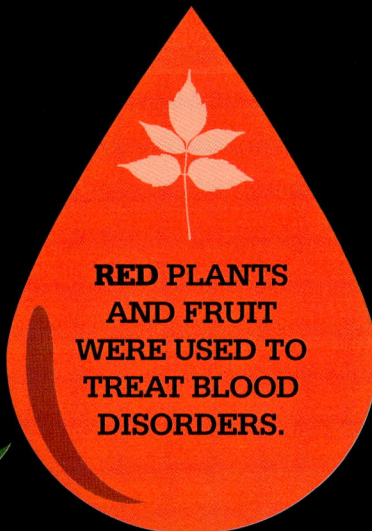

RED PLANTS AND FRUIT WERE USED TO TREAT BLOOD DISORDERS.

YELLOW PLANTS AND FRUIT WERE USED TO TREAT JAUNDICE, A CONDITION THAT TURNS THE SKIN YELLOW.

PEOPLES OF NORTH AMERICA

The Mayans were just one of thousands of native peoples who lived in the Americas. The first people entered the Americas some 40,000–17,000 years ago, crossing a land bridge between Siberia and Alaska. They spread quickly throughout North and South America.

MOUND BUILDERS

For about 5,000 years from 3500 BCE, several cultures built large mounds of earth throughout the Mississippi River valley in the USA. We know little about who these cultures were or why they built these mounds.

THE GREAT SERPENT MOUND, OHIO

NORTHWEST COAST
The **Tlingit**, **Haida** and **Chinook** lived in this region and followed a settled hunter-gatherer lifestyle.

THE PLATEAU
The **Nez Percé**, **Klamath** and other indigenous peoples led a hunter-gatherer lifestyle.

THE GREAT BASIN
Indigenous peoples followed a largely hunter-gatherer lifestyle. They included the **Shoshone** and **Paiute**.

CALIFORNIA
Although some farming was practised in this area, most peoples, such as the **Hupa**, **Pomo** and **Yana**, had a hunter-gatherer lifestyle.

Perhaps the most famous is **Great Serpent Mound,** a snake-shaped earthwork that's more than **400 metres long.**

BEFORE THE ARRIVAL OF EUROPEANS IN THE 16TH AND 17TH CENTURIES, NATIVE AMERICANS HAD DEVELOPED A WIDE RANGE OF CULTURES ACROSS NORTH AMERICA.

ARCTIC

Indigenous peoples included the **Inuit** and **Aleut**, whose way of life developed to cope with the harsh Arctic conditions.

SUBARCTIC

The **Cree, Beaver** and other indigenous people hunted caribou and waterfowl, while gathering berries, roots and sap, and fishing.

NORTH AMERICA

THE NORTHEAST

Many of the indigenous peoples lived in small villages, practising farming. They included the **Algonquin, Iroquois** and **Mohican**.

THE SOUTHEAST

Indigenous peoples included the **Cherokee, Natchez** and **Seminole**. Societies were agricultural and built large earth mounds.

THE SOUTHWEST

Home to both agricultural and hunting societies, indigenous peoples included the **Hopi, Navajo** and **Apache**.

THE PLAINS

Living a largely nomadic lifestyle, indigenous peoples included the **Sioux, Comanche** and **Arapaho**.

SOUTH AMERICA

THE AZTECS

Mesoamerica saw the rise and fall of many other civilisations. These included the Toltecs, the Aztecs and the people who built the huge pyramids at the centre of the giant city of Teotihuacán.

MEGA CITY

By the middle of the first millennium BCE, the city of Teotihuacán was home to about 125,000 people and controlled a large part of Mesoamerica, including many Mayan sites. The city itself is home to two huge pyramids, the Pyramid of the Sun and the Pyramid of the Moon, the biggest built in the Americas.

GREAT PYRAMID, GIZA
146.5 M

PYRAMID OF THE MOON, TEOTIHUACÁN **40 M**

PYRAMID OF THE SUN, TEOTIHUACÁN **75 M**

LAKE TEXCOCO

TEOTIHUACÁN

TENOCHTITLÁN

AZTEC EMPIRE

AT ITS HEIGHT, THE AZTEC CAPITAL OF TENOCHTITLÁN RULED **6 MILLION PEOPLE –** BIGGER THAN THE POPULATION OF DENMARK TODAY.

MEXICO

TOTLEC TAKE OVER

Around CE 900, Teotihuacán was sacked and burned by another group of people from central Mexico, the Toltecs. The Toltecs influenced much of the region for another 200 years, introducing the worship of Quetzalcoatl, the feathered serpent.

THE TOLTECS BUILT RECLINING HUMAN FIGURES, CALLED *CHAC MOOL*.

THE AZTECS WERE A **NOMADIC PEOPLE,** WHO SETTLED NEAR MODERN MEXICO CITY AND **TOOK CONTROL OF A LARGE PART OF CENTRAL AMERICA.** THEY WERE **CONQUERED BY SPANISH EXPLORERS** IN THE **16TH CENTURY.**

CAPITAL CITY

Legend has it that the Aztecs founded their capital, Tenochtitlán, when they saw an eagle, perched on a cactus, attacking a snake. They took this as a sign from their gods that the nearby Lake Texcoco was the site for their city.

THE AZTECS CONTROLLED AN EMPIRE OF MORE THAN

200,000

SQUARE KILOMETRES – THAT'S ABOUT HALF THE SIZE OF THE US STATE OF CALIFORNIA.

THE SYMBOL IS FOUND ON THE MEXICAN FLAG TODAY.

10,000   10,000   10,000   10,000

HUMAN SACRIFICE

The Aztecs sacrificed humans as part of their religious ceremonies. Some stories say that in a single four-day period in 1487, more than

80,000

people were sacrificed.

10,000   10,000   10,000   10,000

A CITY CONQUERED

In 1521, Spanish explorers under the command of Hernán Cortés managed to capture Tenochtitlán and conquer the entire Aztec empire.

THE INCAS

The Incas established their capital, Cuzco, in what is now Peru in the 12th century. They remained a small civilisation for nearly 300 years, before expanding dramatically to govern the largest empire in the Americas.

AT ITS HEIGHT, THE INCA EMPIRE COVERED **2 MILLION SQUARE KILOMETRES** – ALMOST THE SAME SIZE AS THE ISLAND OF GREENLAND.

INCA EXPANSION

From 1438, a succession of Inca rulers expanded their empire in four stages. In less than 150 years it covered a huge area.

COLOMBIA

PERU

ECUADOR

SOUTH AMERICA

BRAZIL

BOLIVIA

PARAGUAY

CHILE

ARGENTINA

1438–1463
REGION CONQUERED BY PACHACUTI

1463–1493
REGION CONQUERED BY TUPAC INCA

1493–1525
REGION CONQUERED BY HUAYNA CAPAC

1525–1532
REGION CONQUERED BY HUASCAR

GET THE MESSAGE

Messengers travelled along the Inca roads carrying messages that were recorded as knotted cords, known as *quipu*.

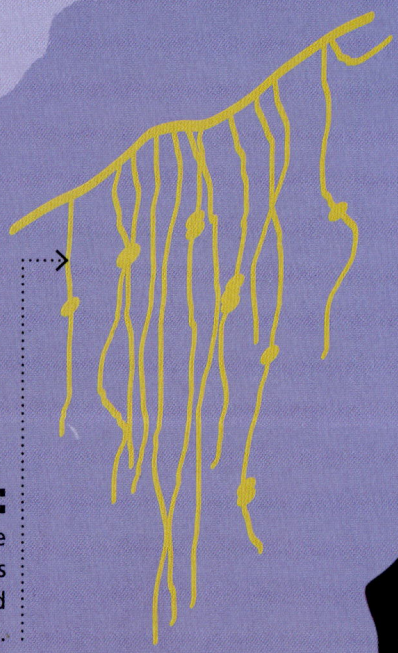

THE INCAS CREATED A TERRITORY THAT RULED OVER 12 MILLION PEOPLE, MORE THAN THE POPULATION OF BELGIUM TODAY.

Inca Empire compared to modern countries
1. Ecuador   15,868,396
2. Senegal   13,975,834
3. Inca territory   12,000,000
4. Belgium   11,323,973
5. Cuba   11,031,43

INCA HIGHWAYS

The Incas built a road network that was more than **32,000 KILOMETRES** long, linking all parts of their empire. It was long enough to stretch seven times across the USA.

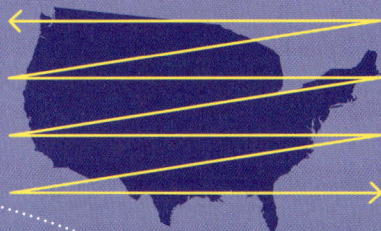

One of these roads ran for more than **3,500 KILOMETRES** along the South American coast – equivalent to four-fifths of the distance between Los Angeles and New York City.

NEW YORK

LOS ANGELES

The Incas built and maintained rope bridges to span the many gorges and valleys in the road network as it ran through the Andes mountains.

WHAT HAPPENED NEXT?

After about CE 900, many of the Mayan cities were abandoned and the civilisation fell into decline. Historians are unsure as to why this happened, but by the time Spanish explorers arrived in Mesoamerica in the 16th century, the Mayans were mainly living in small farming villages.

MAYAN DECLINE

Reasons for the decline of the Mayans include a shortage of water, too many people, clearing of the forest, and the effects of continuous warfare between the various city states.

At the civilisation's peak, Mayan cities may have had a population density of more than

800 PEOPLE

per square kilometre – that's about twice the population density of England.

1 KILOMETRE

1 KILOMETRE

NO WATER

Clearing the rainforest may have increased the effects of drought, decreasing rainfall by up to

30 PER CENT,

because cleared land absorbs less energy from the sun, and prevents clouds forming.

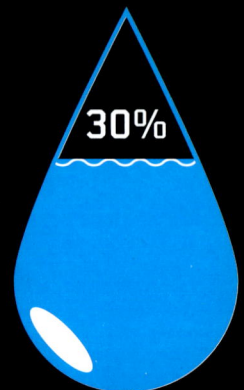

30%

Experts say that
20 TREES
would have had to be chopped down to build every square metre of a Mayan city.

MAYAN REBELLION
During the 19th century, the native Mayans rebelled several times against the government of Mexico.

NORTHERN MAYAN CITIES, SUCH AS CHICHÉN ITZÁ, CONTINUED TO THRIVE AND PASSED UNDER THE CONTROL OF OTHER CIVILISATIONS, INCLUDING THE TOLTECS AND THE AZTECS.

EUROPEAN EXPLORERS AND SETTLERS BROUGHT DISEASES WITH THEM FROM THE OLD WORLD, INCLUDING SMALLPOX, INFLUENZA AND MEASLES. AS MANY AS

90 PER CENT
OF THE NATIVE MESOAMERICANS WERE KILLED BY THESE DISEASES.

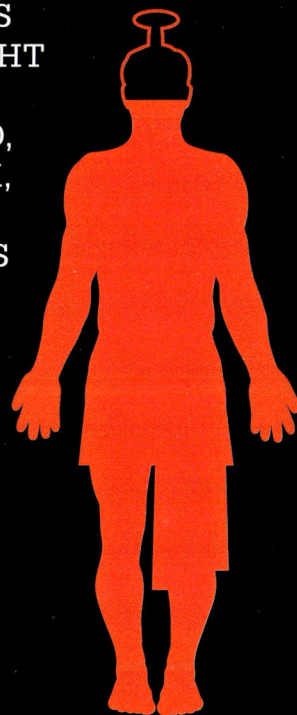

Today, Mayan people live in many of the countries found throughout Mesoamerica. More than **5 million** people still speak one of about **30 Mayan languages**.

GLOSSARY

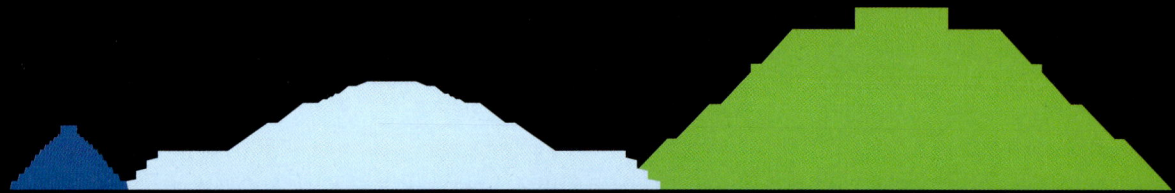

astronomy
The study of stars and other objects in outer space.

atlatl
A throwing stick used to propel a spear with greater force and speed.

Aztecs
A Mesoamerican people who dominated a large area until the arrival of Europeans in 1521.

blood letting
Deliberately cutting someone to release blood, often as part of a religious ritual.

corbel arch
An arch-like structure that uses pieces which stick out more and more until they meet in the middle.

Olmecs
One of the first civilisations to emerge in Mesoamerica. They flourished between 1300 and 400 BCE.

fertile soil
Soil that is very rich in nutrients and will produce good crops.

glyphs
A system of small pictures and images that are used to represent letters, sounds, words or even entire phrases.

hunter-gatherer
A person who gets their food by gathering it from plants and hunting animals rather than farming.

Incas
A people who ruled an empire that covered much of South America until the arrival of Europeans in the 1500s.

independent
Free to do what you want without obeying the instructions of other people.

irrigation system
A network of pipes and channels which carries water to a crop.

jade
A green rock that is sometimes carved to make valuable jewellery and ornaments.

jaundice
A condition which turns the skin of sufferers yellow.

latex
A milky liquid produced by rubber trees, which can be turned into solid rubber.

maize
A tall grass-like plant that produces edible grains that form on its tip.

Mesoamerica
A region in Central America, covering parts of Mexico, Belize, El Salvador, Guatemala, Honduras, Nicaragua and Costa Rica.

obsidian
A dark, glass-like rock that forms when lava cools very quickly.

plaza
Another name for a large open space or square.

reservoir
A store for a liquid, such as water.

sacrifice
To give something up or kill something or someone, often as part of a religious ceremony.

sarcophagus
A large coffin, often made from stone and marble, and covered with images, glyphs and inscriptions.

stelae
Large stone pillars that are often covered with images and inscriptions.

Toltecs
A Mesoamerican people who dominated parts of Mexico from about CE 900–1200.

true arch
An arch formed by placing stones in a curve until they meet at the topmost stone, known as the keystone.

vigesimal system
A counting system based on the number 20.

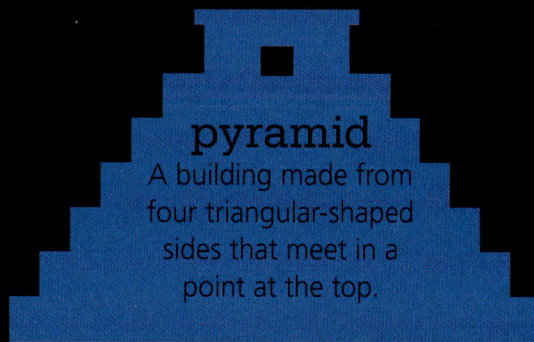

pyramid
A building made from four triangular-shaped sides that meet in a point at the top.

Websites

MORE INFO:
www.history.com/topics/maya
A website that's packed full of facts and videos about the Mayan civilisation, from its very beginning to the present day.

maya.nmai.si.edu
A website from the Smithsonian Institute with information about the Mayan calendar and beliefs as well as teacher notes and resources.

mayas.mrdonn.org
A fun website that's packed with entries and information on a wide range of Mayan topics, as well as online games and clipart.

MORE GRAPHICS:
www.visualinformation.info
A website that contains a whole host of infographic material on subjects as diverse as natural history, science, sport and computer games.

www.coolinfographics.com
A collection of infographics and data visualisations from other online resources, magazines and newspapers.

www.dailyinfographic.com
A comprehensive collection of infographics on an enormous range of topics that is updated every single day!

INDEX

ACKNOWLEDGEMENTS

First published in Great Britain
in 2016 by Wayland
Copyright © Wayland, 2016
All rights reserved

Editor: Elizabeth Brent
Produced by Tall Tree Ltd
Editor: Jon Richards
Designer: Jonathan Vipond

ISBN: 978 0 7502 9839 1
10 9 8 7 6 5 4 3 2 1

Wayland
An imprint of Hachette
Children's Group
Part of Hodder and Stoughton
Carmelite House
50 Victoria Embankment
London EC4Y 0DZ

An Hachette UK Company
www.hachette.co.uk
www.hachettechildrens.co.uk

Printed and bound in China

The website addresses (URLs) included in this
book were valid at the time of going to press.
However, it is possible that contents or
addresses may have changed since the
publication of this book. No responsibility
for any such changes can be accepted by
either the author or the Publisher.

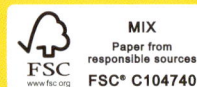

MIX
Paper from
responsible sources
FSC® C104740

GET THE PICTURE!

Welcome to the world of **infographics!** Icons, pictograms and graphics create an exciting form of data visualisation, presenting information in a new and appealing way.

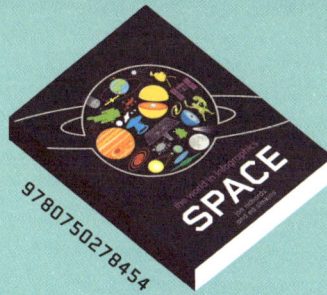

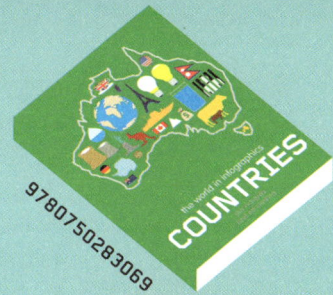

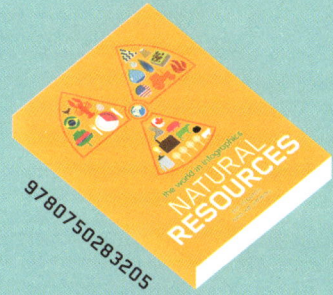

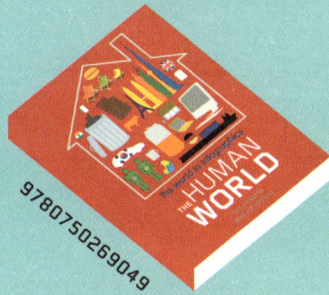

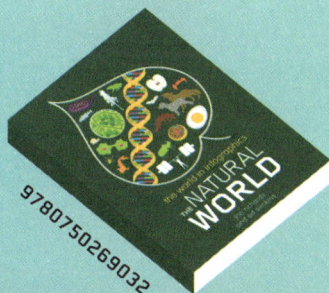

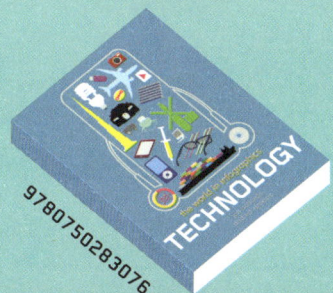

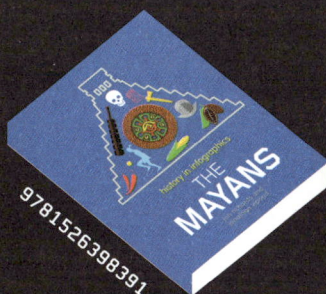

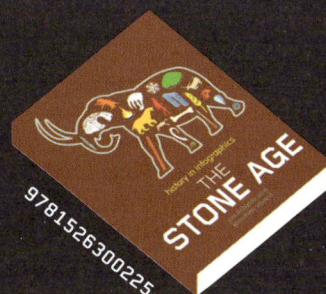

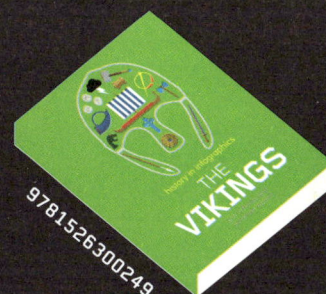

the world in infographics
PLANET EARTH
9780750278461

the world in infographics
SPACE
9780750278454

the world in infographics
COUNTRIES
9780750283069

the world in infographics
MACHINES AND VEHICLES
9780750281287

the world in infographics
THE HUMAN BODY
9780750278683

the world in infographics
NATURAL RESOURCES
9780750283205

the world in infographics
THE HUMAN WORLD
9780750269049

the world in infographics
ANIMAL KINGDOM
9780750283199

the world in infographics
SPORT
9780750277792

the world in infographics
NATURAL WORLD
9780750269032

the world in infographics
ART AND ENTERTAINMENT
9780750279628

the world in infographics
TECHNOLOGY
9780750283076

history in infographics
ANCIENT EGYPTIANS
9780750298407

history in infographics
THE MAYANS
9781526398391

history in infographics
THE STONE AGE
9781526300225

history in infographics
THE VIKINGS
9781526300249